Contents

Introduction

This guide is intended to support students working towards CIE 0486 and 0477. As you know, poetry can be interpreted in different ways, so what I am offering here are some thoughts – absolutely NOT the last word on these poems. Your teacher will introduce you to the poems in a variety of different ways, but it isn't always easy to make all the notes you would like to in class. This guide is back-up. It doesn't tell you how to answer exam questions (although towards the end there are a few hints and some suggested questions to consider) – your teacher will ensure you have all the exam practice you need. Italicised technical terms are explained in the Glossary at the end of the book.

Good luck and enjoy!

Jane Chumbley

The Sea Eats the Land at Home - Kofi Awoonor

Kofi Awoonor was a Ghanaian poet who wrote extensively about African culture and the loss of cultural identity in the face of Western influence.

This is one for the geographers – a poem about coastal erosion. It tells the story of a sea which invades what seems to be a simple, rural community. The sea is 'Running in and out of the cooking places' and on one particular night it 'carried away the fowls,/The cooking-pots and the ladles'. A storm on a cold Sunday morning leaves children shivering, goats struggling and women weeping. Two women in particular are mentioned – Aku and Adena. On this level it is a tragedy: a story of loss, despair and human vulnerability compared to the power of the natural world. The weather wins this battle as the sea 'eats the whole land at home'.

The poem can be interpreted as an extended metaphor for colonisation or for continuing Western influence in Africa, post-colonisation. In this reading, the sea is a metaphor for outside influences which historically sampled and sometimes attempted to dismantle or destroy African culture. So the sea is 'Running in and out of cooking places,/Collecting the firewood.../And sending it back'. Ultimately it's a destructive process and the land (Africa and its inhabitants) suffers. The sea in this poem is ever-present and threatening – 'the eternal hum of the living sea'. In this reading the two anecdotes about Aku and Adena have two distinct purposes. Aku laments that 'Her ancestors have neglected her' and 'Her gods have deserted her' which suggests a loss of faith and cultural values. Adena, on the other hand, 'has lost the trinkets which/Were her dowry and her joy'. This seems to speak of something even more fundamental; despite being trinkets, these cultural artefacts are the most precious things she has and represent both her future and present happiness. Therefore this could be about the loss of cultural identity.

Form and Structure

The poem takes the form of a single unrhymed stanza. It is a *lament*. Although there are no stanza divisions, the poem is structured around repetition of the title; this line occurs four times including a double use at the end where there is some variation. The sea no longer just 'eats the land at home', it 'eats the whole land at home' suggesting a devastating event from which there can be no recovery. There is, therefore, a movement in the poem from what with hindsight looks like minor damage or mischief-making at the start to a full scale catastrophic loss at the end.

Voice and Tone

The story is told by a third person narrator who sees the personal tragedies of Aku and Adena and reports them in a fairly factual, slightly journalistic style, although there is one direct comment when he says 'It is a sad thing to hear the wails'. Otherwise you could imagine you were listening to a television or radio journalist reporting on a recent tragedy and using two anecdotes to add human interest. The slight detachment gives a dignity to the poem; Awoonor lets the repetition and the *personification* of the sea do the work of creating an emotional response in the reader. The tone is factual, muted and respectful.

<u>Language</u>

The language of the poem is very simple and accessible, but there are some subtle points which are worth drawing out.

- *Personification* of the sea – the sea is personified as 'angry' and 'cruel' which gives force to both literal and metaphorical interpretations. In either, it is a force that the local people cannot handle. We could argue that there is no reason for the sea to be angry, that the sea and the land can happily co-exist, that there is no cause for this cruelty. This works for both readings of the poem – in the first, the natural world is mysterious and overpowers humans; in the second, the Western world is predatory and acquisitive, lacking respect for human rights, or it is simply too powerful.
- The *metaphor* of consumption – eating here is about greed.
- Verbs dominate and tell the story – the sea is running, collecting, sending, destroying, carrying away, raging, eating, while the people are calling, shivering, weeping, struggling. Almost all of these verbs are given as present participles which creates an immediacy; we feel as though we are there witnessing these things.
- Sounds – there is the 'lap-lapping of the bark water' while the 'sobs and the deep and low moans' of the people are drowned out by 'the eternal hum of the living sea'. The *alliteration* of 'lap-lapping' complements the *onomatopoeia*. There is *assonance* of the long, mournful vowel sounds in

'low' and 'moans' and further *onomatopoeia* in 'hum'. All these sound effects add a subtle layer of sadness to the poem as it comes to its conclusion.

Themes

- The power of the natural world and human vulnerability
- Loss
- Cultural identity
- Colonisation
- Weather

Prompt Questions

- Does the poem have more or less impact on you if you accept the metaphorical reading that it is about colonisation?
- How does the poet make you feel about the people mentioned in the poem?
- How does the simplicity of the poem add to its impact?

London Snow - Robert Bridges

If you've experienced snow, this poem is a gift. It's so beautifully descriptive that it transports you back to snowy days which never fail to astonish us. What's more, not only is the subject matter easy, the poem is a gift in terms of its figurative language – no shortage here of things upon which to comment! But don't forget to look beneath this beauty; there are ideas and possibly a political reading which make this an even more subtle piece of work. Let's get started...

The story is simple: snow falls during the night on an urban landscape, building to a depth of seven inches. When the Londoners awake, it's bright and silent. The schoolboys scoop up the snow, taste it, make snowballs and shout excitedly. When the adults emerge, it's hard work for them as they trudge, turning the white snow into 'long brown paths', but even they are conscious of the 'charm', the spellbinding beauty which they have broken.

Form and Structure

Bridges is first and foremost a Victorian poet, with this poem written towards the end of the nineteenth century. His London has a recognisable landmark ('Paul's high dome') but the 'traffic' he refers to is horses and carts, not cars.

More importantly for us, though, he's a traditionalist, writing in a very controlled and polished way, using language carefully and precisely. The poem is one long stanza; it's a continuous story. What's less obvious is that it is comprised of only five long sentences, each of them marking a stage in the narrative: the snow falling; the Londoners awakening; the boys playing; the sun stirring everyone; the men emerging to go to work. Each of these sentences can be seen as layered with multiple clauses, mirroring the layering of the snow. The same effect is arguably seen in the rhyme which is regular but very unusual – ababcbcdcdedefefgfgh and so on. It creates an overlapping effect, a kind of woven pattern – delicate but solid, rather like snowflakes compacting.

At the end there is a single long line which breaks the form, just as the men break the 'charm' of the snow.

Voice and Tone

The poem is written in the first person but blink and you would miss the single use of 'I'. The perspective is very detached. Although there is wonder in the poem it does not come from the narrative voice; Bridges does not give us his emotion directly – he points out the eye 'marvelled – marvelled' and the boys 'cried'. He tells us the light was a 'strange unheavenly glare' which was 'dazzling' while the trees were a 'white-mossed wonder'. But never does he tell us directly of his emotions. In doing this he avoids hyperbole and any accusations of sentimentality. He is no Keats and seems to have no interest in *pathetic fallacy* (look it up in the **Glossary**).

The tone, though, is one of admiration and the scene described evokes a sense of the magical. But it is all quite understated.

<u>Language</u>

This poem is a sensual feast, full of *visual and auditory imagery.* Bridges makes extensive use of alliteration, onomatopoeia, metaphor, repetition, personification, adjectival detail and lists. I've tried to group together what I see as the best examples of these: remember when you are writing about a poem that it's never a good idea to just work your way through it, picking things out – look for the bigger picture so you can write about the way the poet is working. However it is true that the figurative language in this poem is particularly dense in the first 9 lines.

- Movement – the falling of the snow is described using multiple verbs – 'flying', 'floating', 'veiling', 'drifting', 'sailing'. These are foregrounded in the first sentence so that the action seems continuous and almost relentless. The words fall like snowflakes perhaps. The verbs are compounded with the adverbs 'stealthily ....perpetually' and 'incessantly', the first of which adds a note of *personification*: the snow is portrayed as secretive and tactical.
- 'Veiling' has a metaphorical quality; the snow obscures London's rough or less attractive edges 'Hiding differences, making unevenness even'. This could suggest an implied criticism of man-made London with its disparate architecture and social divisions – the snow is a kind of equaliser. It could also suggest the power of collective action; a single snowflake achieves very little but collectively

they can put the brakes on a whole city. Alternatively, you could interpret the veil as a bridal image: London is the beautiful bride. This kind of ambiguity is common in poetry about London (see Composed upon Westminster Bridge by William Wordsworth, for example).

- Sound – initially the focus is on the absence of sound, a kind of miracle achieved by the snow as it is 'hushing', 'deadening, muffling, stifling'. The sibilance of 'silently sifting' and 'softly drifting and sailing' creates a softness which is picked up with the alliteration of 'flying..flakes falling..floating' and 'loosely lying'. This is contrasted with the hard alliteration of 'road, roof and railing' – the manmade elements.

- A lexical field of religion is arguably evident with phrases such as 'high and frosty heaven', 'marvelled', 'solemn air', 'wonder' and 'manna'. The 'crystal manna' is a direct allusion to the Bible story in which God provides food for the wandering Israelites in the form of 'manna' – a flake like substance which had to be collected before the sun melted it. Manna was nourishment; it kept the Israelites alive and it was a gift from the Old Testament God. Through this metaphor, Bridges subtly suggests that snow is not only a miracle but that it is somehow essential – perhaps for our spiritual wellbeing. There is no direct reference to religious faith in the poem which is more concerned with Nature and a 'charm' which sounds almost pagan, but this language nevertheless provides a sense of the snow falling being a spiritual experience.

- Contrasts – the contrast of 'white flakes' and 'city brown' is established early in the poem and then repeated at the end when the men 'tread long brown paths'. White has literary connotations of purity and innocence; brown has connotations of things being sullied or dirtied. So the snow purifies and men spoil things. This opposition of Nature and the urban environment/mankind is also seen in the contrasting verbs since men 'Tread...as toward their toil they go', moving heavily and clumsily, like their carts which 'creak and blunder', contrasting the light floating actions of the snow. The contrast is made even more explicit when Bridges says 'war is waged with the snow' although this metaphor of war is not developed strongly. In fact, he seems to pull back slightly with the acknowledgement that 'even for them' (the men) the snow is beautiful and diverting. Despite the poem ending with the word 'broken', the criticism of mankind feels muted, as though Bridges wants us to concentrate on the snow and not the people.

- *Personification* – as well as the stealthy snow (see Movement, above), the sun is personified with 'His sparkling beams' and the air is said to be 'solemn'. In both cases, the natural world is made to seem powerful and important – awe-inspiring perhaps.
- Repetition – 'the eye marvelled – marvelled' and the repetition of the boys' direct speech "O look at the trees!' they cried, 'O look at the trees!'" – in both cases this emphasises the wonder of humans in response to the natural world.

Themes

- Nature, mankind and the urban environment
- Awe and wonder

Prompt Questions

- Do you think Bridges was making a political point about the power of collective action or the way humans impact negatively on the environment?
- The poem captures a moment in time – a transitional moment – we all know the 'uncompacted lightness' of this

fresh snow will turn to dangerous ice or wet sludge. But Bridges shows that people embroiled in their daily lives can still sense the spiritual. Snow has a transformative effect. Is poetry a bit like snow?

Afternoon with Irish Cows - Billy Collins

The first thing to say about American poet Billy Collins is that he's probably not a fan of this kind of literary analysis. You must read his very funny *Introduction to Poetry* (actually a very short poem, not a book) in which he says he wants readers to 'waterski/across the surface of a poem' but all we want to do is 'tie the poem to a chair with rope/and torture a confession out of it'. Unfortunately, that's the difference between reading for pleasure and studying poems for exams. But maybe we should make a special effort to just *enjoy* this poem.

This is a realistic poem about the speaker's encounter with cows. They have been observed, at a distance, on a few occasions, and the speaker seems unsure what to make of them. But 'every once in a while' he is moved to go and see them because of the incredible noise they are making – not a noise of pain, as it turns out, but a cow 'announcing/the large, unadulterated cowness of herself'.

Without actually asking it, Collins raises the question: what is a cow? how can I understand a cow? He said in an interview once that the poem reflected his lack of experience with animals, but he's an observational poet who makes poetry out of everyday encounters, and by the end he has managed to capture something about the 'cowness' of the cow. She is proud, strong, defiant, ancient and ultimately shocking. Despite being so dull she is phenomenal.

Form and Structure

Five seven-line stanzas with no obvious rhyme or rhythm make this a poem which feels even and measured but not constrained or forced. The tone (see below) is conversational which fits; Collins is not setting out to be poetic – he wants to show us something. There is lots of *enjambment* within the end-stopped stanzas which serve as little episodes on a journey of discovery: introduction to the cows; comment on the cows; hearing a noise; investigating the noise; coming to a realisation. So the poem moves steadily towards a kind of epiphany announced at the beginning of the final stanza - 'Then I knew'.

Stanza three is totally enjambed, injecting some pace as the speaker is spurred into action at the 'phenomenal' sound. A similar effect is achieved in the next stanza when he focuses on an extended description of the amazing sound.

Something interesting is happening in terms of time. Collins writes in the past tense ('There were') and says he 'would sometimes' see the cows, suggesting a recurring event in the past. The same thing happens when he says 'Then later, I would open the blue front door'. Hearing the noise is also a repeated event: 'But every once in a while, one of them/would let out a sound'. However, in the fourth stanza he drops the 'would' and seems to be talking about a specific cow – 'the noisy one' – who in the fifth stanza 'regarded my head and shoulders...with one wild, shocking eye'. Reading the poem as a whole, however, there's an underlying sense that this isn't a one-off event, but that he goes on being surprised and having his realisation every time that it happens; it's as if he will never get used to this phenomenon. Perhaps that's why the title is not '**An** Afternoon with Irish Cows'.

Arguably the poem is structured around contrasts – the silence of 'the long quiet of the afternoon' when the cows are 'munching', 'stepping from tuft to tuft' and 'lying down' gives way to 'a sound so phenomenal'...'pouring out'. Similarly, the poet moves from bafflement to realisation. The contrast of human and animal is obviously key to the poem and perhaps we might reflect more on this: is the poem inviting us to compare ourselves to cows which are unashamed and confident in 'announcing' themselves? For more discussion of this, see Language (below).

Voice and Tone

The poem is written in the first person with an informal and conversational tone established with phrases such as 'every once in a while' and 'Yes, it sounded like pain', although there is a sense the speaker is not addressing us directly but rather sorting through his own thoughts. There's a sense of interior monologue when he writes 'How mysterious, how patient and dumbfounded/they appeared in the long quiet of the afternoons' as he briefly moves out of his simple story-telling.

The tone is of someone who is quietly baffled when confronted with a non-hostile alien species whose behaviour seems incomprehensible. He is mildly curious and then, finally, somewhat in awe. The final image of the speaker is slightly ridiculous: the cow 'regarded my head and shoulders/above the wall' and it is the cow who is amazing with her 'one wild, shocking eye'. So we might say there is a tone of humility and slight self-deprecation at the end.

This is, of course, a human perspective on cows. You could try writing from the reverse perspective: what would a cow make of us? See **Creative Challenges**.

Language

Okay, so I don't want to 'torture a confession' out of this poem, but there are some interesting things going on with the language that it's good to admire in passing. In stanza five, for example....

- 'Apologia' – this does NOT mean an apology! Instead it is a formal written defence of one's conduct, a kind of justification. It is an assertion – a confident statement. The cow is definitely not apologising and there is no sense of shame. Rather, she proclaims who she is. Is the poem inviting us to compare ourselves? Despite the cow's very simple life and her limitations (being 'dumbfounded' and 'anchored'), she seems to have a strong sense of identity which we perhaps lack.
- 'Cowness' – this seems a particularly well chosen word – its very clumsiness suggests a quality that it is beyond human description; the cow has an essence beyond human language.

There are five key images in the poem:

- 'the field suddenly empty/as if they had taken wing, flown off to another country' – this *simile* reveals the speaker's bafflement and lack of knowledge of cows. Cleverly, it makes him sound simple whilst making the cows seem dramatic and mysterious.
- 'the black-and-white maps of their sides' – this *metaphor* is visually very effective, a neat way of describing the cows' appearance, but there lurks behind it a sense of the exotic, strange or unknown; the speaker is trying to read the cows much as he might try to read a map.
- 'which one of them was being torched/or pierced through the side with a long spear' – this *hyperbole* again suggests a speaker who is slightly self-deprecatory. His reaction is obviously exaggerated. The idea of the spear is interesting in that it seems to take us back to a savage, pre-civilised world and anticipates the word 'ancient' in the final stanza. Together they seem to suggest the speaker's view of the cow as connected to the past in a long line of cows, all

possessing 'cowness'. Alternatively you might consider the poet is reflecting on mankind's treatment of cows.

- 'the darkness of her belly' – the whole of this extended description is remarkable, using powerful language such as 'bellowing' , 'labouring', 'rising', 'gaping' – but this metaphor seems particularly interesting. 'Darkness' suggests something deep and unknowable, linked to the metaphor of the 'map'.
- 'one wild, shocking eye' – the cow isn't shocked, but has the power to shock us. The poem ends on something of a cliffhanger. You may think there is a sense of latent threat.

Notice also how the landscape is suddenly full of colour for the speaker in the final stanza, as though his discoveries about the cow have made the whole landscape more alive.

Themes

- Nature and mankind
- The extraordinary in the ordinary

Prompt Questions

- If you could only 'waterski across the surface' of this poem, what would you pick out?
- How do humans and cows compare in this poem?

Watching for Dolphins - David Constantine

Dolphins – in Greek literature they symbolise divine protection and guidance; they are seen as the holy animals of Apollo and Poseidon, or as messengers from the gods. Because of their intelligence, they are commonly seen as having a human connection as well as this ancient idea of a divine spark or spirituality.

present and his closing thoughts. Time emerges as an important theme so it's good to be able to link this to structure.

Voice and Tone

The poem is written in the first person and the speaker seems to be a solitary individual who returns to a loved beauty spot after an absence of twelve years. His tone is primarily nostalgic as he remembers the trees fondly and says his 'farewell' before reflecting on his memories. The delicate images he creates (see below) evoke a sense of celebration rather than anger, bitterness or grief. There is a sense of loss but the focus is arguably more on the fact that he has been 'charm'd' by simple rural pleasures in the past.

The tone becomes more philosophical and slightly moralising as he declares 'Short-lived as we are, yet our pleasures, we see,/Have a still shorter date, and die sooner than we', speaking here with the first person plural on behalf of all humankind.

Language

Images of the natural world take centre stage but this is quite delicate – techniques like personification are not overdone and the effect is quite simple and charming:

- Sounds - *onomatopoeia* is evident in 'whispering sound' and the *sibilance* is echoed in the lines that follow - 'The winds play no longer and sing in the leaves/Nor Ouse on his bosom their image receives' – picked up again when he describes the blackbird's song 'Resounds with his sweet-flowing ditty'
- *Personification* – of the trees since they 'lent' him a shade and, perhaps, the winds which 'play; the blackbird is also given a bit of personality as he 'fled to another retreat'
- *Alliteration* - 'cool colonnade' and 'favourite field' are fairly understated, just lending a bit of emphasis. More subtly, alliteration holds together three abstract ideas in the final two stanzas – 'fugitive..fancy..frailty' – see below.

seem to be his concern. It's true that he lists with some sadness the things that are missing now that the trees have gone – the shade, the sound of the wind, their reflection in the River Ouse and the birds which used to sing there – but the poem ends up being about the brevity of human life and pleasure. In other words, he uses the felled trees as a metaphor for human life – we too can be cut down suddenly and with no warning – 'I must ere long lie as lowly as they'.

William Cowper was a forerunner of the Romantic poets such as Wordsworth and Keats (see *Ode to Melancholy*). He was institutionalised for insanity for a short time about 20 years before writing this poem. You should always be cautious about reading too much autobiographical meaning into a writer's work, but it's perhaps not surprising, knowing this background, that Cowper would be sensitive to ideas about 'the frailty of man and his joys'.

Form and Structure

The poem consists of five end-stopped quatrains, each constituting a single sentence. The rhyme scheme is aabb – two pairs of *rhyming couplets* per stanza. The rhythm is slightly varied but often the lines are *anapaestic tetrameter* – in other words, they have four lots of three syllables – an *anapest* is two short or unstressed syllables followed by one long or stressed syllable. None of this is terribly significant except in so far as it shows the poet working within a quite tightly organised frame. There is an elegance, dignity and formality to his writing which suggests calm purpose.

The poem has a simple structure: for three stanzas the poet laments the loss of the trees in a kind of *elegy*. The final two stanzas are more philosophical as the poet contemplates the brevity of his own life and the transience (short-lived nature) of our pleasures.

The poem is also carefully structured in terms of time. The first stanza is in the present, the second in the past, the third in the present, the fourth the future and finally the poet returns to the cast down', emphasising the failure to see compared to the expectation and hope

- *Pronoun shift* – as noted above, the poet uses the third person initially to describe the tourists but later switches to the first person plural, including himself in the group. At that point the dolphins become 'they'. This switch serves to emphasise the gap or gulf between ordinary humans and extraordinary animals – between the prosaic and the spectacular.
- *Symbolism* – the 'chains' of the tankers are a symbol of heaviness and entrapment; combined with the symbolic 'black water' this suggests a loss of hope, a sinking feeling as the tourists return to reality without seeing the dolphins.

Themes

- Hope
- Spirituality
- Nature and mankind

Prompt Questions

- Overall, is the description of people in this poem positive or negative?
- In your opinion, what do the dolphins represent in this poem?

The Poplar-Field - **William Cowper**

You'll read elsewhere that this is a poem about the environment and how we should not cut down trees. I'm not so sure! The title is a bit of a giveway since the focus is not actually on the trees is it? The setting for the poem is a field which prompts the poet to consider the trees which used to grow there and which have been 'fell'd'. He never questions who felled them and that really doesn't

- Piraeus – this is a busy port south of Athens which features in classical literature. In this poem it arguably represents a link between the ancient past of gods and Greek mythology and the present reality of commerce and tourism.
- Aegean – the sea which also features very heavily in Greek mythology and which is frequently depicted as beautiful. Here it is 'abused', again offering a contrast between past and present.
- Satyrs – men with goat features, companions of Dionysus, the Greek god of wine and feasting. Satyrs were lovers of wine, women, pleasure, music and dance. They represent fun and another a connection to the gods. Using a *simile*, 'snub-nosed, domed like satyrs', Constantine adds to the sense that the dolphins have a divine connection.

Religious language is also used although it is delicately laced through the poem so that the ideas feel more subtle. The fat man 'Stared like a saint' suggesting his devotion and his determined, fixed, statue-like stare; the gulls were 'a sign'; all wanted 'epiphany' and were 'praying'; the 'cymbal, gong and drum' are reminiscent of instruments frequently referenced in the Bible in connection with praise and celebration; and the imagined dolphins leap with 'grace'.

Other interesting features include:

- *Ironic juxtaposition* of 'stared like a saint' and 'sad bi-focals' – that poor 'fat man/Hung with equipment' is a bit pathetic in the eyes of the poet isn't he? But don't forget, the poet joins in with him later, aligning himself with the weakly sighted and desperate.
- *Onomatopoeia* of 'clang', 'gong'.
- A *lexical field* of sight is peppered throughout the first half of the poem – noticed, watch, saw, stared, bi-focal, looked, see, gazed – reappearing at the end as 'blinking' and 'eyes

creating what might be seen as wave-like variation. Sometimes the rhyme is used to emphasise key words eg sea-epiphany.

The poem is in three parts. First it tells the story of a recurring event 'In the summer months on every crossing' which is very literal. But in the fourth stanza there is a shift into a more dreamlike sequence where the poet imagines what would happen if they saw the dolphins. The sixth stanza marks a return to the literal – 'But soon/We were among the great tankers...We had not seen the dolphins/But woke, blinking'.

Voice and Tone

The tone at the start of the poem is rather formal and quite detached. The poet uses the detached pronoun 'one', saying 'One noticed that certain passengers soon rose' and 'One saw them lose/Every other wish' which feels slightly disdainful, as though he is looking down on these tourists who he describes as 'hopeless'. However there is a marked *pronoun shift* in the fourth stanza as he enters the dream sequence (see above) and writes 'We could not imagine more prayer', persisting with the first person plural 'we...our' until 'We had not seen the dolphins'. Arguably he then reverts to a more detached ending when he writes that 'the company/Dispersed'.

So he gets involved. His perspective starts as an observer and then he embraces the dream – it's as if he can't resist the pull of the collective wishful thinking involved in this need to see the dolphins. He speaks for the group who are bonded now and no longer individuals – 'a fat man', 'lovers' and 'others [who] looked to the children' – despite the fact they are 'stranger[s]'. It is our dreams and our longing that unite us, he seems to be saying; there is something quintessentially human in seeking a spiritual experience.

Language

The poem contains several *allusions* which need some explanation:

On the face of it, this is a simple narrative poem about the way that tourists in Greece long to see dolphins but end up disappointed. Knowing that dolphins have a symbolic value in literature, however, makes us view the poem in a different light. 'Watching for Dolphins' perhaps means looking for the spiritual, and the poem becomes a comment on that common longing for another dimension in life.

Like so many of the poems in this collection, there are ideas about the way humans collide with the natural world. Here, the people of the poem travel on 'the abused Aegean' sea and merge with 'the great tankers' which pollute with their 'chains/In black water'. The dolphins are not seen. Perhaps the poet is suggesting that the pollution of everyday life makes it difficult to see the spiritual?

Despite this, the poem is about hope and a collective desire for enlightenment – 'All...wanted epiphany' and looked for 'a sign'; when the tourists are 'Hopeless' they 'looked to the children for they/Would see dolphins if anyone would' – presumably because children are less cynical or sceptical and more accepting of the miraculous. The suggestion here is that adults tend to pass on their unfulfilled ambitions to their children. (No pressure there then!). In this sense, the ending of the poem could be seen as sad and *bathetic* (anti-climactic) since no-one manages to see the dolphins. But don't forget that this watching for dolphins happens 'In the summer months on **every** crossing' and 'Day after day'. The desire to see the dolphins seems instinctive as people 'rose' with 'no acknowledgement of a common purpose'. We still believe the dolphins are there, even when we don't see them, and that's faith of a kind.

Form and Structure

There are six loosely rhymed stanzas which flow (like the sea, slightly choppily) from one to the next using enjambment. The rhyme is occasionally full and in couplets (they-day, place-face) but frequently half-rhyme (Piraeus-rose-serious-purpose-bows-lose)

The language used is very simple and straightforward – this is, after all, a poem about simple pleasures. The only complexity comes in the image of 'My fugitive years', a metaphorical use of the word fugitive which usually refers to a prisoner on the run. This subtly suggests that the speaker feels his life is running away from him and that he is a prisoner of time. Through *alliteration*, we can link these ideas to his 'fancy' – his imagination – and his sense of 'frailty': humans are weak and vulnerable, prisoners of their own mortality and unable to hold on to pleasures.

Themes

- Time
- Memory
- Death
- Nature and mankind

Prompt Questions

- Do you think Cowper is advocating 'carpe diem' (seize the day)?
- In your opinion, is the poem about man's destruction of the environment?
- Does Cowper present a conflict or a parallel between man and nature?

You will Know When You Get There - Allen Curnow

Have fun with this. Allen Curnow has reportedly said that the best poems are teasing and that their essence eludes the reader. In other words, they won't spark immediate recognition or understanding. So expect to work hard here if you are looking for meaning. On the other hand, it's a good moment to remember that the primary objective of poetry is to capture moments of experience or thought and create art. Not all paintings are photographically realistic and representative are they? Just as you can like a particular corner of a painting and recognise the fact the painter has used oils, for example, so too you can appreciate a particular image in a poem and acknowledge the poet's technique. It's not all about meaning.

Having said that, it's human instinct to search for meaning and you'll want some starting points for your own investigations. So here goes.

The poem's title is also the title of the collection in which it appeared in the early 1980s and it signals that the work might be about journeys which are inevitably a metaphor for self-discovery. The story in this poem concerns a man walking down to the sea to pick mussels, late in the day and late in the season, pretty much as the sun sets. The path is 'steep' and 'wet-metalled' from a recent rain shower. He is 'alone' although there are two boys having a campfire who turn their faces towards him. This fragment of story is buried in descriptions of the light which is arguably the main subject of the poem as the poet refers to it directly four times.

The poem contains some amazing metaphorical description and Curnow uses some really intriguing adjectives and verbs which make the poem sparkle (see Language). Don't forget to enjoy these, even if you find the poem difficult! Some ideas about possible meanings do emerge as you work your way through the language.

Form and Structure

The poem is organised in ten unrhymed couplets and a final stanza where a single word spills over onto a third line. Only the final stanza is end-stopped and there is a lot of enjambment in the poem, sometimes strategically used to create pace such as when he writes about the light 'which keeps//pouring out of its tank in the sky' or a deliberate delay when the light 'lasts//over the sea'. There is a fluidity to the poem which reflects the fluidity of the light he is describing but conversely, the use of couplets also creates a slightly jarring effect as though these are notes or jottings – moment by moment observations that haven't entirely gathered into a whole yet. Despite being end-stopped, the final statement 'Down you go alone, so late, into the surge-black/fissure.' supports this idea that the story isn't over. An ominous note is sounded with the word 'alone' and the intensifier 'so'. A fissure is a split, crack or chasm (see Language).

Voice and Tone

The poem is not obviously written in the first person because there are no first person pronouns – no I, me or my. But the poet uses direct address twice – 'down you go' and 'Down you go alone' – and also refers to the way two boys look at 'this man going down to the sea'. The phrasing of all this allows the possibility that the poet-speaker is, in fact, describing his own experience in the present tense - viewing it in a slightly detached way and seeing himself from the boys' perspective as a 'man'.

With this in mind the opening lines 'Nobody comes up from the sea as late as this…and nobody else goes down' sound slightly self-critical, and the idea that the man has 'an arrangement with the tide' is ironic and humorously self-deprecating: the speaker is creating humour at his own expense – who has an arrangement with the tide and such a pedantic one at that – for 'the ocean to be shallowed three point seven metres'? In fact, the image of 'this man going down to the sea with a bag' also starts to look slightly comical, particularly against the magnificent backdrop of 'the earth rolling back and away'. At the very least, he looks inadequate in comparison.

The language in this poem is frequently very creative. It's not a romanticised vision of the world and the lack of an obvious first person speaker means there is no direct emotional response. Instead the imagery often seems very robust. Some examples include:

- Interesting verb choices - 'a shower passed **shredding** the light', 'the moon **sponging** off the last of it' and 'the sea-floor **shudders**'. 'Shredding' encapsulates the idea of an interplay between the rainwater and the light – the moisture affects the way we see the light, breaking it up, creating lines and layers. The verb to sponge is rather colloquial and therefore quite arresting in this poem where the language is mostly quite formal. To sponge off someone is to scrounge. Is the moon scrounging light off the sun? In one sense, yes. But I think there is a more literal sense in which the moon is absorbing light, like a sponge. When the sea-floor shudders we feel the reverberation. The shudder could describe the heaving, shifting movement of the sea-floor in response to the 'heavy wave' in which case it's a great verb – just think how pathetic the verbs ripple or shake would sound in comparison! But there's also a hint of personification isn't there, just as there was with the sponging moon? Here it gives us a sense of the sea-floor feeling some repulsion or even fear. It's not a happy emotion and perhaps begins to support a reading of the natural world's antagonism towards this mussel-picking man.
- Interesting adjectives – '**Too/credibly by half celestial**', '**campfirelit** faces' and 'the **excrescent** moon'. Celestial is ambiguous since it can refer to the sky and all things astronomical, or it can mean heavenly, divine, godly. The phase 'Too credibly by half' feels like it should be

hyphenated (like a Gerard Manley Hopkins compound adjective – see *The Caged Skylark*, below) – so it would read too-credibly-by-half. It's a very conversational way of saying something is absolutely beyond doubt believable. So is he affirming the divine source of the light? Or just emphasising that the light pours from the sky? The adjective feels too elaborate to be the latter. The adjective to describe the boys' faces has that same quality of a compound but with the hyphens removed and the words elided (merged). The adjective used to describe the moon – 'excrescent' – has the sense of bulging, swollen or popping; the idea is that the moon is growing excessively. What he is describing, of course, is not an increase in size so much as an increase in presence – the moon becomes stronger as the sun sets, as it sponges or soaks up the sun's light in a kind of trade. Featuring the adjective at the line end gives it prominence which is exactly the effect of the moon at this moment in the poem.

- Interesting metaphors – 'the light which keeps/pouring out of its tank in the sky' and 'the dammed reservoir up there keeps emptying'. These metaphors go together and both describe the sun as a storage facility, with the light as its liquid contents. This is what I mean by robust imagery – it is strong and impactful but not delicate. The first use of the metaphor features in a lovely long sentence which pours much like the light it describes 'through summits,/trees, vapours thickening and thinning'.

- Interesting images – 'the surge-black fissure' and 'the light lasts/over the sea, where it 'gathers the gold against it''. The poem's closing image is, as noted above, rather ominous. The steep path is no longer lit by the sun but is surge-black, like the sea. The onset of night seems a little threatening as does the idea of going down into a fissure – a crack or a chasm. The other, earlier, image is much more positive.

Curnow seems to be quoting (or misquoting?) a poet from the early twentieth century, Ezra Pound, whose Canto XI has the line 'in the gloom, the gold gathers the light against it'. Pound's image is a metaphorical one of hope in times of despair. On one level, of course, Curnow is discussing light more literally so he describes here the way the light seems to glow richly on the sea. It would be the most beautiful and poetic image in the poem but its impact is less because of the quote marks. It's almost as if Curnow is suggesting it is a bit cliché.

There is one final mysterious image bridging the final two stanzas where 'A door//slams, a heavy wave, a door, the sea-floor shudders'. It's hard to see this as a literal door since there are no other references to manmade things in the poem. So we could see this door as a metaphor for the heavy wave – a metaphor which Curnow explains and then curiously repeats. Door slamming isn't just about force and power, it speaks of anger and of closure, of locking someone or something out. There's a note of hostility here and – as noted above – the sea 'shudders' suggesting it does not welcome the sun setting or perhaps the arrival of the mussel-picking man. But down he goes, on his journey. Whether he comes up again we aren't told...

Themes

- The natural world and mankind's place in it

Prompt Questions

- What's your response to the idea that the best poems tease the reader?
- How does this poem make you feel?
- What is the poet suggesting about the natural world – the sun, the moon, the sea?
- Why is the sea shuddering?

The Caged Skylark - Gerard Manley Hopkins

To understand this poem you need to know that Gerard Manley Hopkins was a devout Catholic – a Jesuit priest - who believed in the resurrection of the body: after Jesus returns, we will get back our bodies that we lost at death, but they will be transformed and free from any pain or suffering.

This poem is an *extended simile* comparing a caged skylark with the 'mounting' human spirit trapped in a heavy body, 'his bone-house, mean house'. Although both skylarks and humans have moments of happiness in life, the poet says, there is lots of suffering – 'bursts of fear or rage'. But being raised by Jesus at the resurrection will be like a bird being set free. Just as the skylark still needs his 'nest', now it is a home to him, not a 'prison'. Similarly, the poet says, humans will need bodies but they will be 'uncumbered' – light, not limited, not weighed down.

The poem is an argument for the doctrine or belief in the resurrection of the body. It's a piece of persuasive writing, designed to explain the doctrine in accessible terms through comparison with something we can all understand – a bird, a cage and a nest. There is no plot.

Form and Structure

In essence this poem is a *sonnet*, although not usually printed as a single stanza. It has two quatrains which make up the *octet* and rhyme abbaabba and two tercets which make up the *sestet* and rhyme ccdccd. It is traditional in a sonnet for the octet to introduce an idea which the sestet may reverse or develop. We see that here: the poet introduces the idea that both the skylark and the human spirit are caged, before he explores the freedom enjoyed by the uncaged bird and the human spirit after it is set free (in the resurrection of the body). So the structure is of confinement/oppression and freedom/liberation.

Gerard Manley Hopkins rejected traditional rhythms involving regular patterns of stressed and unstressed syllables. He used something he described as *sprung rhythm* instead. Essentially this involves a varying number of syllables (one to four) with the stress always falling on the first syllable. In practice, this is similar to free verse and gives his writing a spontaneous quality.

Voice and Tone

The poem is written in the third person using masculine pronouns for both bird and human. The tone is one of conviction – clear belief – and argument. Notice the way some of the lines begin with what we might call discourse markers in English Language – 'Yet..Or..Not that...But..But' – words that mark out the progress or stages of the argument. The only burst of emotion comes when the poet writes 'Why, hear him', using an imperative (command) which again suggests that desire to persuade. There is an essential energy in the voice which comes through the repetition – such as 'sweetest, sweetest', 'sweet-fowl, song-fowl', 'hear him, hear him' and 'own nest, wild nest'. Perhaps we can just see this as Gerard Manley Hopkins in his Jesuit priest role, urging faith and understanding on believers.

Language

You'll have noticed that the poet uses a lot of hyphenation. He creates a lot of compound adjectives such as 'dare-gale' or compound nouns such as 'sweet-foul' or compound verbs such as 'day-labouring-out'. This compresses his ideas and creates an intensity – sometimes making it difficult for us to grasp the meaning on first or even second or third reading. It's worth spending some time with these compounds. For example, 'dare-gale' compresses the idea of a skylark who risks high winds, while 'day-labouring-out' is a really heavy (or laboured, hah!) way of suggesting that life consists of a daily repetition of the hard, physical work endured by people hired on a daily basis for little reward; we day-labour-out our life on earth.

Hopkins also loves sound – particularly *alliteration* – which floods his poetry and sometimes creates particular effects. For example, the heavy alliteration of harsh d and b sounds in the octet mimics the 'drudgery' being described. Sometimes the alliteration holds together two important ideas – for example, the 'skylark scanted'; having foregrounded the description of the skylark as 'dare-gale' this is then strongly juxtaposed by the word which now sticks to the skylark through alliteration – 'scanted' means treated inadequately or limited.

The *imagery* of the cage mentioned in line one is dotted throughout the poem with 'cells', 'barriers' and 'prison', making a *lexical field*.

The image of the 'rainbow' mentioned in the final line needs some explanation. Hopkins says that the meadow is not 'distressed' when a rainbow appears or has its 'footing' there. There is an implied *simile* here: we won't be weighed down or distressed by our resurrection bodies. The rainbow has special significance within Christianity though, since it is a Biblical *symbol* for hope and God's promise (God promised Noah that He would never again allow floods to destroy all life and the rainbow would be a reminder of that promise).

Themes

- Oppression and freedom
- Death
- Nature and mankind

Prompt Questions

- How does the extended simile help readers to understand a complicated idea?

- Is Christian faith required to appreciate the ideas in this poem?

In Praise of Creation - Elizabeth Jennings

This poem is about 'order' and 'rule' in the natural world. As the title suggests, the speaker writes in an act of praise which has echoes of religious faith since the word 'creation' implies belief in a creator. Elizabeth Jennings was a devout Catholic and known for her religious vision. Here, though, such beliefs are only subtly implied as her focus is almost entirely on the natural world – the birds, stars, tigers, sky, moon and the way they behave 'to rule'. For example, 'the birds mate at one time only'. It is only in the final line that she refers to man and there is no direct reference to a creator, only to 'order' and the sense of guiding principles that she sees in the sky and in animal instinct.

The focus on the tiger suggests a connection with William Blake's eighteenth century poem *The Tyger* which also includes reference to skies and stars as well as the tiger's eyes. Blake is much more direct in questioning who made the tiger but speaks of the animal's 'fearful symmetry' which feels like a forerunner to Jennings's idea of 'order'.

Form and Structure

There are five stanzas of four lines each, all rhyming abab – so the form reflects the order and perfect balance that is her topic. It's a simple and quite formal style of writing which gained popularity in the second half of the twentieth century as something of a reaction to the experimental free verse of the modernist poets who wrote in the early decades.

The poem begins with a sense of awe as though the speaker is suddenly struck with a realisation – 'That one bird, one star,/The one flash....Purely assert'. The repetition of 'one' is an important structural element as it is here that she establishes both the simplicity and magnificence of the point she wants to make: just one bird or one star or a single tiger is enough to prove ('testify') without any kind of fuss ('ceremony') that there is 'order' and 'rule' in creation.

The second stanza is about explanation. Repetition or listing is used here to a similar effect: 'How the birds mate...How the sky is..'. The listing suggests there are lots of ways she could prove this point to you but her illustration is vague and rather unscientific as she speaks about 'a certain time' and 'sometimes' in relation to changes in the sky or moon.

The third and fourth stanzas – the only two which are enjambed – are where she drills down to the single example of the tiger mating. This is much more elaborate although again, romanticised and unscientific. Of course, she is exploring the irrational – mating is instinct for animals – so maybe being unscientific is appropriate.

The final stanza is also linked to this episode in that it begins with a post-coital (after sex) 'quiet' but develops out into other images of rest – 'birds folding their wings' (perhaps after a long flight), 'The new moon waiting' and 'The season sinks'. The final line is surprising – mankind has not been mentioned at all until this moment. Of all beings in creation, it is 'Man' who rests 'with his mind ajar'. And so the poem ends with the beginning of a new thought: for all that the world works on principles of order and animal instinct 'beyond reason', it is humans who possess the capacity for rational thought. The surprising ending is challenging and should make us think.

Voice and Tone

The poem is written in the third person; despite this the tone is one of awe and conviction (she believes and asserts confidently) – in part conveyed by the early repetition but also by the passionate and intense imagery of the third and fourth stanza – for example the image of the tiger waiting 'For the blood to pound, the drums to begin'.

<u>Language</u>

There is a string of great metaphors in the third and fourth stanzas, all of them centred around the tiger:

- The tiger is 'trapped in the cage of his skin' and the metaphor here seems to be a way of neatly suggesting the tiger's stripes – they look like the bars of a cage – but also the way the tiger's intensity is locked up within him. His heavily patterned skin perhaps acts as a warning to other creatures that he is dangerous, but that danger is contained within him.
- The tiger waits for 'the drums to begin' and for the 'tigress' shadow' to cast 'a darkness over him'. The drums here are a metaphor for the thrilling expectation of mating – perhaps an accelerated heartbeat - while the 'darkness' is a metaphor for the way the female brings out the male's sexual drive. This metaphor is very nicely developed on this line as 'A darkness over him, a passion, a scent' with each of these additional phrases acting like a quick breath or pant.
- 'The world goes turning, turning' could be a metaphor for sexual climax but has some other value. On one level it serves to bring us back to the other elements of the natural world she listed earlier – the moon, sky, stars. These elements keep 'turning' regardless of other activity on earth. It's also possible this is slightly cheeky reference to a poem by W B Yeats called The Second Coming written in the aftermath of WW1 and painting a rather pessimistic view of the way events were spinning out of control – it begins 'Turning and turning …things fall apart'. Jennings suggests

the complete opposite of course; in her view, the world turning represents security, order and purpose.

The final metaphor of the poem is about mankind. Writing that man's mind is 'ajar', Jennings suggests the image of a door that is half open. Having an open mind is actually a very clichéd metaphor, but this is a powerful image upon which to end the poem; she seems to be suggesting that if we have an open mind, we of all creatures are capable of rational thought and we should be able to see that there is order and purpose in creation. These things, she seems to say, cannot exist without the guiding hand of a divine creator; if you have an open mind you will see it. There is an irony here, of course: we can reason but some things – like faith – are beyond reason.

Themes

- The natural world and mankind
- Religion
- Order and purpose

Prompt Questions

- Is Christian faith required to appreciate the ideas in this poem?
- What similarities can you find between this and *Stormcock in Elder*?

Ode on Melancholy - John Keats

Melancholy is a feeling of gloom and sadness. Today we might think of it as a kind of depression. Writers in the seventeenth and eighteenth century were a bit obsessed with it, producing brooding melancholic characters or exploring in very precise detail what caused the condition. Here, Keats gives his solution: embrace it, accept it, but don't act on it. This is probably one of the toughest poems in the collection but stick with it because Keats does actually have a point and you might recognise his idea as something you've experienced.

It helps to start at the end because it's not until the third stanza that Keats explains his thinking. The essence of his argument is that all beautiful, lovely, wonderful things are short-lived. So it's inevitable that they lead in the end to sadness (or melancholy). Pleasure and pain go together, he says. But it's precisely because beauty and joy are transient (short-lived) that the experience of them is more thrilling and intense. You can't have joy without sadness; only by experiencing sadness do you appreciate joy. So far, so good – or at least, it makes a kind of sense although it's a sad truth.

His solution – which comes in stanza two – is to throw yourself into beauty – 'glut thy sorrow on a morning rose' and 'feed deep, deep upon [thy mistress's] peerless eyes'. That way the sadness you feel will be particularly intense. This bit is harder to accept but Keats and the other Romantic poets romanticised these intense feelings, whether happy or sad. They wanted to feel things intensely. And that might be something you can understand.

The poem starts with Keats telling us not to take drugs, contemplate suicide or focus on death because we will stop being alert – 'For shade to shade will come too drowsily,/And drown the wakeful anguish of the soul'. Instead, we should focus on beautiful things – the 'morning rose', 'the rainbow of the salt sand-wave', 'the globed peonies' or a lover's 'peerless eyes'. The reason for this is that 'Beauty must die' and 'Melancholy has her sovran shrine' in the 'temple of Delight'. Our aim should be to 'burst Joy's grape' – experience exquisite pleasure and pain, one after the other.

Keats's Death Gallery
Stanza one reads like a list of exhibits in a museum focused on death. Here's a quick guide:
Lethe: in Greek mythology, the river of forgetfulness bordering the underworld
Wolf's bane: poisonous plant
Nightshade: poisonous plant
Proserpine: from Greek mythology, the Queen of the Underworld – she was allowed to return for sixth months of the year, bringing Spring
Yew-berries rosary: yew-berries are symbols of mourning; yew trees are often planted in graveyards; a rosary is a string of beads
Beetle: probably a scarab beetle; ancient Egyptians put these in tombs as a symbol of resurrection but for Keats they are a symbol of death
Death-moth: thought to represent the soul leaving the body at death, but also featuring markings rather like a human skull
Downy owl: owls are nocturnal and therefore associated with night, death and being otherworldly

Form and Structure

An Ode is a formal Greek verse written to praise or defend someone or something. The tight organisation of Keats's three 10-line stanzas makes this Ode seem very formal. It's also very logical, as an argument should be: don't do this (stanza 1), do this instead (stanza 2), here's why (stanza 3). Whether you agree with the argument is another matter! The poem begins *in media res* and quite strikingly (see below). In fact, when Keats first wrote the poem there was an opening stanza in which someone is clearly trying to assemble a boat, perhaps to sail on the river Lethe. He discarded this and the poem is more subtle and impactful as a result.

The rhyme is also very tight: all three stanzas are divided into two rhyme groups – a *quatrain* of abab and a *sestet* of cdecde or cdedce. The sestet in some measure develops what has been introduced in the quatrain.

The rhythm is similarly very organised: Keats uses *iambic pentameter* (10 syllable lines organised into five groups of two syllables – one unstressed, one stressed – diDUM). Occasionally this is reversed (eg 'Sudden from heaven' where 'Sudden' is DUMdi and the emphasis is placed on the first syllable to give impact) or altered altogether – most notably in the stunning opening line 'No, no, go not to Lethe' where both the first two syllables are surely stressed, with a follow up iam placing another stress on the third negative word out of four.

Voice and Tone

The poem is not written in the first person which is perhaps a bit surprising since it's obviously written from a position of personal experience. But the focus here is on instruction; there is direct address to the reader – 'Make not your rosary of yew-berries' – and the tone is first urgent 'No, no, go not' and then patient as Keats explores his idea giving multiple examples to help the reader understand. The poem concludes with astonishingly beautiful images and the tone is almost triumphant – 'His soul shall taste the sadness of her might,/And be among her cloudy trophies hung.'

Language

Imperatives dominate the first two stanzas. In stanza one they are overwhelmingly negative – 'go not...neither twist...nor suffer...Make not...Nor let' – whereas in stanza two they are focused on action – 'glut...Emprison...feed'. The imperatives stop when Keats explains himself in stanza three – which fits with the structure (see above). The negative language in stanza one is very intense and forceful.

Classical *allusions* are used fairly liberally (see Keats's Death Gallery). Proserpine is a particularly useful character for Keats because she embodies both joy and sadness: joy when she returns and brings Spring, sadness when she is compelled to go back to the underworld.

There are several key images, several of which embrace opposition or contradiction, sometimes in the form of *oxymoron*. The reason is clear: Keats is talking about the fusion of two opposites - joy and sadness - so he mirrors this in his images, forcing us to feel that these oppositions can co-exist.

- 'thy pale forehead to be kiss'd/By nightshade, ruby grape of Proserpine' – two contradictions: kiss and poison followed by poison and beautiful jewel-like fruit. The images are delicate and shocking at the same time.
- 'a weeping cloud,/That fosters the droop-headed flowers all' – rain is sad or miserable, making the flowers droop, yet it 'fosters' or nourishes them; rain is essential for fertility and life.
- 'an April shroud' – the clouds and rain form a veil – a shroud is a clear reference to death since it is a cloth draped over a dead body. April is a month of contrasts – sun and showers (joy and sadness).
- 'the rainbow of the salt sand-wave' – no contradiction here but think about it, the glimpse we get of the colour spectrum in a wave is incredibly brief – a flash, and it's gone. On the other hand, there will always be more waves, won't there?
- 'aching Pleasure' – an *oxymoron*.
- 'Turning to poison while the bee-mouth sips' – this compressed image is of a bee sipping nectar from a flower which suddenly becomes poisonous.

- 'cloudy trophies' – an *oxymoron*, surely, since trophies gleam and shine.

> Fun Fact
> Keats trained to be an apothecary – like a pharmacist. That's probably why he is so sharp with the references to poisonous plants – Wolf's-bane and nightshade.

Themes

- Transience of beauty and inevitability of sorrow
- Time

Prompt Questions

- Is Keats advocating 'carpe diem' (seize the day) or something a bit different?
- Is this really a poem about how to cope with sadness – or something else?
- How do Keats's classical allusions contribute to the effect of the poem?

Coming - Philip Larkin

This early poem by Larkin, written when he was a young man in the late 1940s/early 1950s, is what he described as a 'single shot' at a 'sharp, uncomplicated experience'. The story is simple: one evening towards the end of Winter a thrush sings, heralding the start of Spring, and the speaker feels happy like a child. It's a simple story and you'll enjoy writing about this; it has a great combination of techniques that are easy to understand and ideas which you can recognise. But it's also more subtle than it seems on first reading. It's a deceptively clever little poem.

Form and Structure

With its short lines and single stanza, this looks like the 'single shot' that Larkin described, doesn't it? Most of the lines have five syllables but this isn't a rigid form – it's designed, surely, to feel spontaneous. Two shorter lines stand out and between them hold the essence of the story: 'A thrush sings' and 'Feel like a child'. There are three sentences – the first two run over four or five lines and finish with a reference to the houses. The subject matter here is very physical – the houses, the gardens, the thrush, the trees. The third sentence is longer, much more abstract and personalised – an imagined voice, a memory and a feeling. This movement from the concrete to the abstract is typical of Larkin – a poet who, rather like Billy Collins (see *Afternoon with Irish Cows*), deals in the everyday but makes us think more deeply about mundane experiences.

The poem is also structured in terms of time: beginning in the present, the thrush predicts the future and the speaker thinks back briefly to his past before returning to the present. We are left in the present because that's where the pleasure is, but that pleasure rests on a promise of the future – the 'Coming' Spring.

Voice and Tone

This poem is written in the first person although the speaker doesn't reveal himself until the final part of the poem. Despite this, we learn quite a lot about him in a short space of time: he's observant, he was bored as a child and he has the capacity to respond instinctively to the natural world. The tone is soft, quiet and gentle. Even the repeated 'It will be spring soon' is not exuberant or excited – it's the imagined voice of the thrush (hence the repetition, to suggest the repeated notes of a birdsong) and therefore insistent rather than frenetic. The fact that he only 'starts to be happy' is significant: he's not wild with excitement but has a glow building inside.

Larkin is expert at selecting small, telling details and this poem is no exception, despite its brevity. His scene-setting is subtle:

- Seasonal references – the evenings are 'longer', the garden is 'bare' and the thrush's voice is 'fresh-peeled' as we are moving out of Winter.
- Adjectival detail - the evenings are 'light, chill and yellow' – a triple of adjectives that combines *visual and tactile imagery* along with repeated light 'l' sounds; the thrush's voice is 'fresh-peeled', a metaphorical compound adjective which makes me think of a ripe apple, something incredibly clean and raw.
- *Personification* – of the houses which have 'serene/Foreheads' and brickwork which is astonished. He makes the houses sound solid and comforting which provides a good contrast to the delicate light and the trilling birdsong. The line 'Astonishing the brickwork' is, in itself, astonishing or arresting – it stops us in our tracks. The value of these short lines is evident here – the phrase becomes very prominent because it occupies its own line. The thrush's song must be a powerful thing to impact so strongly on the solid, heavy brickwork!
- *Symbolism* – the thrush may have been surrounded by laurel trees but laurel leaves also have a symbolic value in literature where they are often seen as representing prophecy, creativity and poetry. This feels very appropriate. Surrounded by laurels, the thrush predicts 'It will be spring soon' and creates beautiful music which prompts a poem to be written – prophecy, creativity and poetry.

The last eight lines of the poem are an *extended simile* – this experience is compared to that of a child 'Who comes on a scene/Of adult reconciling'. The word 'reconciling' is carefully chosen as it stands out from the otherwise very simple lexis of the poem; it is polysyllabic and abstract. Reconciling means making-up. What the poet doesn't say directly – because it would disrupt the mood of the poem – is that for there to be a reconciliation there must have been a dispute. Lurking behind this simple story of hope there's the shadow of an unhappy childhood of parental arguments where laughter was 'unusual'. As a child, though, he didn't need to 'understand' this adult world in order to feel happy – irrationally happy – when the parents were laughing. The extended simile is very poignant as well as effective in helping us to understand the spontaneous, irrational, almost grateful nature of his happiness now that Spring is 'Coming'.

Don't miss the irony of remembering a 'forgotten boredom'. This is typical of Larkin – he throws in a little tease, something for you to puzzle over. Is he mocking himself? Are these painful memories he has tried to forget and now calls boredom so he can appear offhand and casual? Given the extended simile that follows, it's tempting to create a whole, sad history for this young man and feel even more acutely his pleasure as he is able to appreciate something so simple as the thrush's song.

Themes

- Spring
- Time and change
- Happiness
- Hope
- Children and adults

Prompt Questions

- Does the word 'starts' in Larkin's final line undo some of the poem's happiness for you?
- Which is your favourite image in the poem? Why?
- Is this poem predominantly about Nature or mankind?

Stormcock in Elder - Ruth Pitter

This poem is part of a long tradition of poems which focus on birds (*The Eagle* by Alfred, Lord Tennyson and *The Darkling Thrush* by Thomas Hardy are two clear forerunners to this offering). It's a familiar topic and tends to produce similar ideas – comparisons between birds and humans or awe at the majesty of the natural world - but Pitter manages to put something of her own twist on it. The story is straightforward: the speaker is hiding away in a ramshackle building when, through a hole in the roof, she hears and sees a stormcock singing. She describes the bird in detail before demanding to know 'How you can make so brave a show', reflecting on the fact we can't really understand half of the world and then instructing the bird to 'sing your song and go your way'.

What is a Stormcock?
Stormcock is the commonly used name for the Mistle Thrush. The name is given because of this bird's tendency to sing in all weathers. In fact, according to the RSPB, it is actually 'stimulated by approaching storms and will sing or call lustily before and through bad weather'. Towards the end of the poem the speaker refers to the bird as 'hard-times braggart' – he shows off when it gets tough. Knowing this could be a key to interpreting the poem. Of course it's a poem about a bird, but it could also be about the way some people are able to embrace bad fortune and sing their way through it, whilst others – like the speaker – hide away in a 'dark hermitage' with a 'broken roof'.

Arguably, the poem ends up being about the contrast between responses to dark situations; the bird sings and the speaker hides in a dark place.

Form and Structure

The poem has a very traditional feel: seven 6-line stanzas all rhyme ababcc. Pitter is not an experimental poet. There is a linear chronology to the narrative, and the poem is structured so that after the initial introduction and scene-setting, the focus shifts to the bird. In the second, third and fourth stanzas the poet only uses personal pronouns (I, my) four times; in the fifth stanza she disappears from the poem entirely, so strongly is she focused on the description of the bird. She reappears briefly in stanza six but only to demand something from the bird – 'tell me'. So the structural shift to the bird shows us a speaker taken out of herself entirely for a moment in time. The poem ends with reflection.

Voice and Tone

The poem is written in the first person and although we learn very little about the speaker (see above) there are hints of a back story. For example, she begins 'In my dark hermitage' and 'aloof', with this word left hanging at the end of the line, suspended before the enjambment kicks in and we read that she is aloof 'From the world's sight and the world's sound'. A hermitage is a religious retreat and aloof means detached. So she's on a kind of spiritual holiday from the world, perhaps to devote time to prayer and contemplation. That makes sense, as she is obviously a thoughtful, observant person – the stormcock is described in great detail and the encounter makes her reflect on human life.

But is 'dark' to be understood literally or metaphorically? The hermitage has a 'small door' and later in the stanza she 'groped along the shelf' so maybe there's not much light. However, a metaphorical reading would suggest she's in a dark place – she's withdrawn from company and she's a bit lost emotionally. At the end of the poem she is unable to explain how some people feel joy - 'One-half the world, or so they say,/Knows not how half the world may live' - and she sends the bird away. 'Aloof' can also mean cool, distant, uninvolved or unfriendly. There's no human connection in this poem, although she feels the energy of the bird intensely - signalled with repetition in lines such as 'How strongly used, how subtly made' and the triple patterning of 'The scale, the sinew, and the claw' which gives a driving rhythm to the verse. She also signals in the first stanza that this is 'celestial food' to her – a kind of gift from God perhaps. But at the end she's left with 'elder-spray by broken tile' and a 'broken roof' which gains significance by being mentioned more than once (see below for more discussion on this).

So I would say the mood of the poem is ultimately a little bleak, although definitely ambiguous. The tone of the speaker's voice is harder to pin down – reflective, appreciative, curious but ultimately a little dismissive? This is one where you definitely need to make up your own mind! (See **Creative Challenges**).

Language

A lot of language points are included in the discussion above but it's worth looking closely at some of the description. Contrast is effectively established between the very simple lexis used to describe the hermitage – 'dark.. small... old... broken' – and the elaborate extended description of the bird. But contrast is also seen within the description of the bird as the poet suggests the bird finds joy in unlikely places. For example in stanza 2

- 'wintry glee' – wintry suggests cold, frosty, harsh, unpleasant – yet it is combined with glee which is joyful
- 'The old unfailing chorister' – old yet determined and full of song.

Elsewhere the description is unfailingly positive

- Sound effects – plosive sounds are used effectively in the line 'Burst out in pride of poetry' with the stress falling on the first word very powerfully to mimic the sense of bursting out.
- *Imagery* – different parts of the bird's body are detailed – the 'throbbing throat', 'the breast dewed', 'the large eye, ringed with many a ray', 'the feet that grasped the elder spray', 'the flight-feathers...white/Merged into russet'. In

each case the language is carefully chosen (*alliteration*, interesting verb choice, *alliteration, symbolism* – see below, colour *imagery*) but this all comes to a head in the intense fifth stanza where the description of the feathers spills over almost *hyperbolically* with repetition of 'bright' and the *metaphor* of 'Gold sequins' which combined with the 'shower/Of silver' suggests a richness. 'Like a brindled flower' is a bit of an anti-climactic *simile* at the end (brindled means streaks of brown). The *imagery* of the fourth stanza is reminiscent of William Blake's poem *The Tyger*.

- *Symbolism* – the elder-spray may refer to the branch of an elder tree. The elder is sometimes seen as a symbol of energy, life and creativity, perhaps because it grows rapidly. This is entirely appropriate for the stormcock who has 'grasped' this energy and has a creative attitude to bad weather. Alternatively 'elder-spray' may be a reference to ground elder which is a fast-growing, invasive weed that crowds out other plants. If so, the stormcock has grasped the weed triumphantly and is not put down. The weed could be a metaphor for life's problems which crowd out joy. In grasping the weed the stormcock rises above it, singing in spite of the problems. Either works.

- *Metaphor* – the speaker uses several *metaphors* for the stormcock, notably that he is 'Soldier of fortune' suggesting a hardy, attack-and-defence attitude. Referring to the bird's song (or lungs) as 'your bagpipes' suggests a loud, insistent powerful sound.

- *Simile* – the speaker also likens the bird to 'a rich merchant at a feast' which links with the bird's gold and silver plumage and implies richness of spirit as well as pleasure. It links back to the 'celestial food' mentioned in the first stanza. Rather than the simple 'bread' she was looking for in her hermitage, she found a feast – but is it the bird who is enjoying the feast? The speaker also says the bird is 'as bright as Gabriel', a reference to the angel Gabriel from the Bible, presumably. Gabriel brought good news (to Mary, mother of Jesus) – so maybe the poem does finish on a positive note after all, as he is able 'to smile/On elder-spray and broken tile'.

I want to come back to the 'broken roof'. The speaker says 'through the broken roof I spied' and later 'Plain through the broken roof I saw'. This is understood on a literal level – the roof had a hole and it was through this that she saw the bird. But could it also be seen as a *metaphor* for her state of mind? The house is a fairly common *metaphor* for the human body, with the attic as the brain. So despite her fragile or broken state of mind, the speaker is able to see the bird and recognise the beauty and joy he embodies. The question is, can she share it?

Themes

- Hope; joy in adversity
- Nature and mankind
- Beauty of the natural world

Prompt Questions

- Is it important to know the religious faith or state of mind of the poet in order to appreciate this poem?
- How can a poem have two distinctly different interpretations?

Cetacean - Peter Reading

Cetacean refers to marine mammals such as whales, dolphins or porpoises. In this case, the creatures being described are Blue Whales. Using this more technical term – which could be understood as a noun or an adjective – is an interesting starting point for appreciating what is going on in this poem. The poet takes a fairly anti-romantic stance towards the amazing Blue Whale and the detachment begins with the title. It's technical, relates the Latin order name *Cetacea* and feels very, well, biological. It speaks of classification rather than admiration. And it sets the tone for the whole poem which is almost prose-like in its very, very factual - almost dull - account of an encounter with a group of blue whales. (Imagine what your teacher would say if you handed in a piece of imaginative writing with those sentence starters – 'Out...They...They...Then...And then...Then...Then...'). That's not to say I think the poem is dull – far from it. It's fascinating.

The speaker describes the encounter very precisely in terms of place, time, speed, distance and angles. What he doesn't describe are his feelings or those of anyone else. In fact, no other human is mentioned despite the first person plural of 'our vessel' and 'we did' in the first stanza. The focus is very much on the whales as specimens to be observed. The poem is a record of that observation with details precise enough for the reader to be able to visualise the scene.

It's worth taking a moment to do just that. Having told us the 'vessel' is 'some sixty-three feet', we are then told the whales are 'about twenty feet longer' – so 83 feet. Or 25 metres. That's something approaching the length of a school basketball court. If you go to the National History Museum in London you will be able to see a blue whale skeleton of this size in the foyer. It's enormous. The height of its blow – 'thirty feet' – would hit the ceiling of your school sports hall. Surely no-one can fail to exclaim in amazement?

Yet there is nothing of that in this poem. That's fascinating.

Form and Structure

The poem comprises seven end-stopped stanzas – all but one contains a single sentence, all but two are spread over three lines.

There is no discernible form or pattern. It feels oddly like disjointed prose or the jottings towards a short story that didn't develop. And in a way it is that lack of development that makes it a poem – a moment in time captured in few words with much left unsaid.

After the introductory stanza which sets the scene in terms of place (very precise – 'Fisherman's Wharf, San Francisco... off the Farallones'), time (quite precise – 'Sunday, early') and purpose ('to observe Blue Whales'), the focus is entirely on the rise 'at a shallow angle' and fall 'at a shallow angle' of the whales. The repetition of this phrase creates a sense of completion and a natural end to the poem. It does not matter what the humans said or did, whether the water was choppy or whether they were home in time for brunch. Somehow, the simplicity of the form and structure manages to convey the sense that nothing humans can say or do matters very much in comparison. The narrative – such as it is – is cut short as soon as the whales disappear.

Voice and Tone

The poem is written in the first person but there is no use of the first person singular 'I', 'me' or 'my', meaning that there is no sense of a personal response. Having referred to a group with the plural 'our' and 'we' in the first stanza, humans are not mentioned again. It's hard to deduce any tone at all from the poem. You could say it is factual, unemotional, detached and almost flat. It feels at times, as with the form, that the voice reveals a deliberate attempt to downplay what must have been an amazing sight. Yet very cleverly perhaps what is not said, says it all. This sight does not need to be dressed up; the facts speak for themselves. Alternatively, you might argue that the poet is reluctant to praise the whales; he refuses to sentimentalise as so many other poets might have done (consider other poets and poems in this collection) – either because he does not wish to be like everyone else or because he takes a scientific view of the animal kingdom, or because he wants to challenge us to think about our own response a bit more. Other poets guide us; he doesn't.

Language

As well as the title, correct technical terms are used to describe aspects of the whale eg 'dorsals' (the small fins three-quarters of the way down the whale's back), and 'flukes' (the whale's tail).

The two *similes* in the poems likewise have a precise focus. The whales were 'grey as slate' and their blows were 'as straight and slim as upright columns'. The speaker wants us to see the colour and see the angle/size and uses inanimate objects as comparison – there is no attempt to convey mood or tone.

Measurements of time, speed, size, distance and angle dominate the poem eg in stanza two 'slowly...shallow angle...tiny and stubby... broad flat...one quarter'.

The writer refers to the whales using the third person pronoun 'they' until the final stanza where they are called 'the creatures'. Again there is that lack of attachment; 'creatures' is arguably quite a cold word and it seems no connection has been established as a result of the observation. The speaker went 'to observe Blue Whales – and we did' just that.

Themes

- The natural world
- Human response to the natural world

Prompt Questions

- Does the poet admire the Blue Whales? How do you know?
- Is this a poem?
- Does this unsentimental response to the natural world appeal to you more or less than other poems eg *Stormcock in Elder*?

The Buck in the Snow - Edna St Vincent Millay

This is a strange little poem which has at its heart a single event: a pair of deer – a buck and a doe – stand in the orchard, leap over the stone wall and into the wood; the buck falls and dies while the doe continues running. He is dead; she is alive. The whole event is observed by the speaker who says 'I saw them. I saw them suddenly go' and who challenges the white sky 'Saw you not...the antlered Buck and his doe..?'. The speaker uses the event to consider 'How strange a thing is death' and 'How strange a thing...[is] Life'. No conclusions are reached beyond that.

<u>Form and Structure</u>

The poem is just 12 lines long and organised into three stanzas of five lines, one line and six lines. The single line stanza is clearly the structural pivot and heart of the poem – 'Now lies he here, his wild blood scalding the snow' - a startling image that demands attention (see Language, below). The rhyme is centred around the repetition of 'snow' and matching long o sounds such as 'doe...go...slow' but we are jolted out of this pattern when the buck is brought 'to his knees, ...to his antlers'. The fact that the rhyme is re-established for a final couplet about the doe who survives suggests that the rhyme is intended to be *mimetic* – in other words, it reflects the meaning. Rhyme is life; disrupted rhyme is death. Alternatively, you could say the rhyme is broken or interrupted like the life of the buck.

The poem moves from narrative to reflection, and from past to present, a move which is reflected in the speaker's tone (see below). This shift is supported in the syntax which becomes a little convoluted in the final stanza with multiple *caesurae* slowing the pace generated earlier on.

Voice and Tone

The poem is written in the first person with direct address to the sky. The speaker's tone initially seems a little fierce with a slightly accusatory style of questioning – 'Saw you not…?' she asks before continuing assertively 'I saw them. I saw them' with the repetition conveying her energy and passion. She is appreciative of the deer – shown in the way she describes their 'long leaps lovely and slow', but the single line announcing the death of the buck is starkly delivered – she isn't obviously mournful or passionate. Her words seem calculated to shock, to stop us in our tracks: 'Now lies he here, his wild blood scalding the snow'.

Language

The setting is depicted using careful *imagery.* The sky is described as 'white' to match the snow and *symbolically* suggest the purity of the natural world. This is then starkly contrasted with the image of the buck's 'wild blood' which, it is implied, stains the pure snow. However the poet uses a *metaphor* for greater impact when she writes of 'his wild blood scalding the snow'. The image here is of heat and burning which provides the contrast with the cold of the snow and arguably achieves a stronger sense of something wrong; it is a *paradox*, after all, because snow cannot be burned can it? So, she implies, the buck should not have died here and now.

There is another layer of *symbolism* at work in the poem, however. Not only are the sky and snow white and pure, but the 'apple orchard' suggests a Garden of Eden, with the buck and doe as Adam and Eve characters. Leaving the garden has resulted in the death of the buck, but not the doe. How strange, the poet says. Perhaps she is commenting here on the randomness of life and death. Perhaps when she asks the sky 'Saw you not..?' she is in effect asking a divine power why He or She has not intervened. How strange.

The natural world seems to weep a little in response to the death of the buck – as the hemlocks 'Shift their loads a little, letting fall a feather of snow'. The *metaphor* of a feather of snow is very delicate, rather like the 'long leaps lovely and slow' of the deer.

What are hemlocks?
The hemlock trees are conifers – they look like very bushy Christmas trees. They are not poisonous, unlike hemlock plants. Don't get them confused.

Themes

- Life and death – the fragility of life; the sudden transition from life to death
- The natural world

Prompt Questions

- Is it significant that the doe (female) survives? Edna St Vincent Millay was a feminist.
- Is this poem predominantly about Nature or mankind?

Written Near a Port on a Dark Evening - Charlotte Smith

This is a very descriptive *sonnet* infused with a heavy, brooding and rather ominous feeling. Arguably the real subject of the poem - 'life's long darkling way' - isn't signalled until the very end. The poet first introduces us to the dark scene signalled in the title - the night is 'dark' and 'All is black shadow' - before drawing attention to the light - a 'line/Marked by the light surf on the level sand' and the 'ship-lights [which] faintly shine'. This then sets up the idea that these lights trick or mislead people just like 'wavering reason' misleads people enduring the hardships of life.

Form and Structure

This is one of very many *sonnets* written by Charlotte Turner Smith in the second half of the eighteenth century. The sonnet has 14 lines divided into an *octet* of 8 lines and a *sestet* of 6 lines. The octet sets up an idea that the sestet develops: here the octet sets the dark scene and the sestet describes light in relation to the darkness. Here Smith uses the Shakespearean sonnet rhyme scheme of ababcdcdefefgg. Historically the sonnet was used for love poetry but Smith is not alone in turning it to other subjects. In fact, she wrote an extensive sequence of 'Elegiac Sonnets' which are mournful (an *elegy* being a lament for the dead).

Voice and Tone

The poem is written in the third person with no sense of the speaker conveyed. The tone is brooding – suggested by the dark imagery and the opening phrase which personifies the natural world – 'Huge vapours brood' while the billows are 'drowsy' and the night is 'mute'. There are references to people – the seamen and the pilgrims – but they are not characters.

Language

Light in literature usually represents clarity or understanding. We use this *metaphor* when we say something throws light on a situation. Here, though, the poet complicates and almost reverses the idea. Although initially the light created by the white surf breaking on the shore is described as 'lucid' suggesting reason and clarity, the ship-lights are 'Like wandering fairy fires, that oft on land/Mislead the pilgrim'. The *simile* here suggests the lights are a fantasy or false. So they trick people on land and end up being the opposite of helpful. This sets up another level to the *simile* – 'Such the dubious ray/That wavering Reason lends' – suggesting that if we doubt then we can easily get led off in the wrong direction. Exactly what she means depends on the phrase 'wandering reason'. A

Christian might interpret this as a sonnet about religious faith; if your faith in God doesn't hold strong then you will go off down the wrong path. A rationalist might interpret this as a warning to always apply reason to judgements, to think things through carefully.

With the setting of a port and the multiple references to the 'ocean...billows...surf' and 'ship...bark...seamen' the idea of life as a journey is a central *metaphor* which emerges in the final line as 'life's long darkling way'. The fact that life is 'darkling' picks up the *imagery* of light and dark which has been so powerfully present in the poem.

Sound is also very important in the poem – with reference to the ocean being 'mute' except for the 'repercussive roar'. The *alliteration* here is picked up in the 'rugged foot/Of rocks remote' which gives a hard edge to counter the *sibilance* of 'ocean settles' and 'drowsy billows' reflecting the contrast between land and sea.

So the whole poem plays with contrasts or oppositions – light and dark, sound and silence, hard and soft, land and sea, true and misleading, certain and uncertain – faith and doubt, perhaps.

Themes

- The natural world
- Faith

Prompt Questions

- Is it important to know the religious faith or state of mind of the poet in order to appreciate this poem?
- What sense of beauty is created in this depiction of the natural world?

The Kraken - Alfred, Lord Tennyson

If you've seen *Pirates of the Caribbean: Dead Man's Chest (2006)* then you are on home territory here. If you haven't, think monster and think big. The Kraken is a vast and ancient sea monster from Norse mythology – a bit like the Loch Ness monster but bigger – the size of a Norwegian fjord according to some sources. Of course its existence is a myth, but Tennyson's interest was possibly spiked through the discovery of several dinosaur skeletons in the early part of the nineteenth century, around the time he was writing. He may also have been influenced by the Biblical description of a Leviathan in the book of Job which made its way into the epic poem *Paradise Lost* by John Milton. That's more than enough background – if you can picture a giant squid you're probably near enough. The point is that Tennyson seems to have been a bit taken with the Kraken. The poem isn't about fear and danger, though. It seems to be more about awe and respect. In fact, he appears sympathetic. When he explains that the Kraken will die as soon as he emerges from the ocean, it seems a little sad, we've been so impressed by the creature.

So the poem is descriptive. Tennyson describes the Kraken sleeping deep below the surface, with 'huge sponges' swelling above him and 'enormous polypi' (jelly like creatures) fanning him. He's been 'battening' or stuffing himself with 'huge sea-worms' whilst he sleeps. With three lines to go, there's some action: Tennyson describes what will happen when 'the latter fires heat the deep' – in other words, come Doomsday, the end of the world or the apocalyptic event referred to in the Bible as the 'latter days' – the Kraken will rise up 'roaring', be seen once by men and angels and then die on the surface of the ocean.

Does it mean something? Critics have put forward lots of suggestions. First and foremost it's a piece of fantasy writing; Tennyson enjoyed drawing on mythology (check out *Ulysses*, which is a great dramatic monologue using characters from Homer's *Odyssey*). If you're inspired by fantastical literature, why wouldn't you contribute to the genre?

On the other hand, there are some readings which seem very valid. Here we go with some favourites:

- The poem is about the fact that we live in the dark – uncertainty or gloom – we will only be enlightened or relieved of our burden at the point of death. It's true Tennyson lived at a time of great uncertainty, produced largely by the scientific advances of the time, although ideas about evolution didn't strongly emerge until well after this poem was written. It's also true that Tennyson suffered from depression following the death of his great friend Arthur Hallam, but again this was after this poem was written.
- The poem is about the fact that we bottle up our feelings which will only die when they final express them. In this reading the Kraken is a *metaphor* for destructive, unhelpful emotions.
- The poem is about the artist who needs to hide away from the world if he or she is to produce great work. If the artist is exposed to the world, creativity will die. This is an idea that Tennyson arguably explores in his much longer poem *The Lady of Shalott*. The reading is more obvious there than it is here, as the isolated Lady of Shalott weaves a beautiful tapestry by looking at a reflection of the world in a mirror. When she turns to look at the world face to face – in fact she turns to look at the lovely Sir Lancelot – then the mirror cracks from side to side. She leaves her tower, gets in a boat, floats downstream and dies.
- The Kraken is a *metaphor* for the working class who are oppressed by the dark forces of industrialisation. At a critical moment in time they will rise up but they will not survive

their own revolution. This is a particularly popular reading as England had escaped the bloody revolution seen in France towards the end of the previous century, yet writers like William Blake (who died only a few years before Tennyson wrote *The Kraken*) were very conscious of social forces and working class oppression. Tennyson, being part of the elite establishment, might reasonably have respected and sympathised with the working class without wanting them to have a successful revolution.

Most of all, I think it's a piece of fantasy writing.

Form and Structure

The Kraken is written in the form of a *sonnet* although an unconventional one since it has 15 lines instead of the normal 14 and a pretty odd rhyme scheme as well. Seen like this, it's possible to argue that the form reflects the content – like the Kraken it is a unique, twisted, monstrous, odd and unpredictable creation. However, I think there is something a bit more subtle going on. For example, the rhyme marks out a kind of octave with ababcddc (normally you'd expect ababcdcd or abbacddc, but we'll let that pass), leaving seven lines instead of the normal six. So the extra line is in the second part of the sonnet, rhyming efeaafe. This is the part of the poem that describes the Kraken emerging from the sea – he breaks out of the ocean just as his poem breaks out of the *sonnet* form. The repeated a rhyme also helps to emphasise those repeated words - 'deep' and 'sleep' - which are the focus of the poem until the Kraken emerges.

Voice and Tone

This poem is written in the third person with only the briefest of direct references to mankind in the penultimate line where Tennyson writes that the Kraken will rise 'once by man and angels to be seen'. On the face of it the poem is not about people. The tone is one of mystery, awe and some excitement .The final line sounds quite triumphant when 'In roaring he shall rise'.

<u>Language</u>

The poem deals with extremes in terms of depth/size, sound and time. There is also a *lexical field* of mystery.

- Not only is 'deep' repeated but the sea is described as 'abysmal' where the primary reading must be like an abyss, although it may also have connotation of something appalling and terrifyingly awful. The Kraken is 'Below' and 'Far, far beneath'; sponges and sea-worms are 'huge'; while the 'unnumbered and enormous' polypi have 'giant' arms.
- Sounds – after 'thunders of the upper deep' (a reference to the noise of the surf), there is no sound at all until the final line and the Kraken's onomatopoeic 'roaring': both are huge sounds.
- A *lexical field* of time includes 'ancient', 'millennial', 'ages', whilst a *lexical field* of mystery includes 'shadowy', 'wondrous' and 'secret'.

<u>Themes</u>

- Mystery
- Death

<u>Prompt Questions</u>

- What do *you* think the poem means?
- How does the poet feel towards the Kraken?

Creative Challenges

Producing your own creative responses to poetry is a great way to get into the themes, ideas and style of the verse. It's possible such work could double up as coursework for an IGCSE English Language qualification. If not, it will be good practice for the writing (both fiction and non-fiction) that you have to do in your Language exams. Some of the non-fiction tasks might be the basis for a Spoken Language or Speaking and Listening presentation.

1   The *Sea Eats the Land at Home*: Research the history of colonisation in Ghana and prepare a presentation for your class.

2   *London Snow*: Write a news report for the breakfast news bulletin (radio or television) or the late morning edition of the newspaper about the heavy snowfall overnight. Include quotes from interviewees. What will you choose as your angle – traffic chaos or beauty? As an extra challenge, use as many nouns from the poem as you can.

3a   *Afternoon with Irish Cows*: Write from a cow's perspective: what would she make of us humans? Use details from the poem eg I saw him come out of the blue door

3b   *Afternoon with Irish Cows*: Over the course of 24 hours write down a list of at least 20 moments that could be turned into poems. You don't have to write the poems (although you could) – this exercise is about being alert to the ordinary like Billy Collins. Rather than write a single poem on a single moment, you could pull them all together under the title *Extra-ordinary Life*.

4   *Watching for Dolphins*: Write your holiday blog as if you were a tourist on the boat entering Piraeus. Research the port and the Aegean; find out about the myths in which they feature. Use

details from the poem – perhaps you are the fat man or one of the lovers! Explore your feelings about the way everyone seemed so desperate to see the dolphins. Why did you care so much? How did you feel at the end of the journey? Would you sign up for another boat trip?

5 *The Poplar-Field*: Find or draw a picture of a poplar tree. Decorate it with phrases from the poem. Add your own 'whispers' – what would the tree say?

6 *You will Know When You Get There*: Imagine you are a travel writer who has been commissioned to produce a guide to the coast in a certain area. Write the entry for this stretch where there are several steep paths down to a chasm-like cove. It's a great place to watch the sun set and the moon emerge. Sometimes locals go there to pick mussels. Read some travel writing before you start to pick up the style: first person, past tense, personal account interwoven with facts, description and observation (advice from the The *Guardian* newspaper).

7 *The Caged Skylark*: Research and compare other poems written about skylarks (eg *To a Skylark* by Percy Bysshe Shelley. Find all the recurring ideas and use these words/phrases to decorate a picture of a skylark.

8 *In Praise of Creation*: If you have a religious faith, write a short article for the school magazine called 'Some things are beyond reason' in which you defend your faith. In it you must argue that humans are rational beings and yet some things are beyond reason, hence faith. Refer to the examples Jennings uses.

9 *Ode on Melancholy*: Imagine you have been asked to contribute to a self-help guide for teenagers. Write the entry for a chapter called 'Coping with sadness'. If you like Keats's ideas then use them. If you don't, then include your thoughts about them in a section called 'Dealing with unhelpful advice'.

10	*Coming*: Write a long, thin poem which is a 'single shot' at a 'sharp, uncomplicated experience'. Combine this with 3b if you are short of ideas for a starting point.

11a	*Stormcock in Elder*: Stage a debate in class around two opposing ideas – This poem is bleak and This poem is hopeful. Gather evidence from the poem to support your view. Read *The Darkling Thrush* by Thomas Hardy and make parallels with this poem which support your case (it will work for both sides!).

11b	*Stormcock in Elder*: Read *The Darkling Thrush* by Thomas Hardy. Imagine you are Ruth Pitter. Write a letter to Hardy explaining how you used his poem for inspiration. Make sure you use quotations from both poems. Explain how you developed or diverged from his ideas. Alternatively, imagine you are Thomas Hardy. Write a letter to Ruth Pitter. Might you complain that she has stolen your ideas? Or will you praise her for the quality of her description? What questions will you ask her about her spiritual state of mind? Pitter was a Christian and Hardy abandoned his faith.

12a	*Cetacean*: Write two versions of the sub-text to this narrative ie what the speaker is thinking but not saying. The first version has him being entirely dismissive about the whole episode – he is a scientist or a bored viewer and he will not be impressed. The second version has him in absolute awe. Which do you prefer? Which is more plausible? Evaluate your work and justify your conclusion with close reference to the poem.

12b	*Cetacean*: Research facts about the Blue Whale and prepare a presentation for your class.

13	*The Buck in the Snow*: Write from the perspective of the doe. What were you and the buck thinking when you left the apple orchard to leap over the stone wall? What are you thinking now? Try to use as many words from the poem as you can.

14   *Written Near a Port on a Dark Evening*: Write a companion poem or piece of prose called *Written Near a Port on a Bright Morning*. Use Smith's poem as a model but establish all the contrasts – so 'Night on the ocean settles dark and mute' could become 'Daybreak on the ocean shimmers bright and busy'.

15   *The Kraken*: Re-write the poem so that it is about the Loch Ness monster or another mythological sea-creature. Replace all the descriptive words with your own eg 'Below the ripples of the glassy lake…..'. Invent your own mythology for when, where and with what consequences the creature will emerge.

Exam-style Questions

1   How does Awoonor powerfully present ideas about loss in *The Sea Eats the Land at Home*?

2   Explore the way Bridges vividly creates a scene in *London Snow*.

3   How does Collins use the cows to explore interesting ideas in *Afternoon with Irish Cows*?

4   Explore the way Constantine's poem powerfully conveys ideas about the way humans interact with the natural world in *Watching for Dolphins*.

5   How does Cowper powerfully convey the speaker's feelings in *The Poplar-Field*?

6   Explore the way Curnow uses phrases for striking effect in *You will Know When You Get There*.

7   How do Gerard Manley Hopkins and Ruth Pitter use the image of a bird to explore interesting ideas in *The Caged Skylark* and *Stormcock in Elder*?

8   Explore the way Jennings develops interesting ideas about the world in *In Praise of Creation*.

9   How does Keats explore memorable ideas about sadness and joy in *Ode on Melancholy?*

10   How does Larkin convey powerful feelings of hope in *Coming*?

11   Explore the way Pitter uses striking language to describe the bird in *Stormcock in Elder*.

12   Explore the way Reading memorably presents the whales in *Cetacean*.

13   How do the poets use images of death to explore ideas about life in *The Buck in the Snow* and *The Poplar-Field*?

14   How do the poets vividly create settings in *Written Near a Port on a Dark Evening* and *You will Know When You Get There*?

15   How does Tennyson create a strong sense of mystery and danger in *The Kraken*?

Assessment Criteria

To do well you will be expected to

- make a perceptive, convincing and personal response
- show a clear understanding of the text and its deeper implications
- respond sensitively and in detail to the way the writer achieves his/her effects
- Integrate a lot of well-selected reference to the text

Exam Hints

1 Break down the question – be clear that you will have to address WHAT and HOW (the content and the way the poem has been written) – the question will often direct you to a theme (eg conflict, beauty, power) and focus you on style (eg powerfully presents/vividly creates).

2 Plan – make sure your plan has clear points about the topic so that you can show your understanding of the poem's content

3 Support all your points with quotation – multiple quotation if possible

4 Stylistic and language comment should accompany the quotation

5 Explore effects – the impact on the reader or the different interpretations that might be possible

6 Create paragraphs that have the following shape:
   POINT - responding to the question focus
   EVIDENCE - quotation
   DISCUSSION - effect/interpretation/naming technique
   Your teacher may have an alternative version of this PED structure – be guided by your teacher.

Glossary

Alliteration: term used to describe a series of words next to or near to each other, which all begin with the same sound. This creates particular sound effects eg *a hairy hand, the luscious leaves.*

Allegory: like metaphor – a story told in simplified form but with hidden meaning. The component parts represent something else.

Allusion: a reference – a classical allusion is a reference to a story from Ancient Greece or Rome.

Ambiguity (noun), **ambiguous** (adjective): (from the Latin for 'doubtful, shifting') the capacity of words and sentences to have double, multiple or uncertain meanings. A **pun** in the simplest form of ambiguity, where a single word is used with two sharply different meanings, usually for comic effect. Ambiguity may also arise from **syntax** (when it is difficult to disentangle the grammar of a sentence to resolve a single meaning), and from **tone** (where the reader cannot tell, for example, whether a text is to be taken seriously).

Anaphora: repetition of a sequence of words at the beginning of consecutive lines.

Antithesis: opposite

Association or **Connotation:** a word can suggest a range of associations and connections in addition to its straightforward dictionary meaning. For example, *heart* has many associations with love, courage and other human values, besides its literal, biological meaning.

Assonance: repetition of identical or similar vowel sounds in neighbouring words. It is distinct from rhyme in that the consonants differ while the vowels match eg *Shark, breathing beneath the sea/Has no belief, commits no treason.*

Ballad: songlike poems with a strong story.

Bathos: anti-climax. Bathetic is the adjective, meaning anti-climactic or disappointing.

Caesura: plural caesurae – a pause

Connotations: associated ideas

Dialogue: words spoken by two or more people in conversation.

Direct speech: words spoken and shown in speech marks eg He said 'I have been crying' (see Reported speech).

Elegy: formal lament for the dead

Emotive language: language that provokes a strong emotional response.

Enjambment: where lines of poetry are not stopped at the end, either by sense or punctuation, and run over into the next line. The completion of the phrase, clause or sentence is held over.

Epigraph: short quotation or saying at the beginning of a poem or story, intended to hint at its meaning.

Euphemism: (from the Greek for 'speaking fair') unpleasant, embarrassing or frightening facts or words can be concealed behind a euphemism: a word or phrase that is less blunt, rude or frightening than a direct naming of the fact or word might be. Hence 'to kick the bucket' is a euphemism for death. Sexual functions, death and body parts are typically disguised in this way in common speech.

Exclamative: exclamation

Figurative language: language which is not literal – it relies on *figures* such as similes and metaphors

Foregrounding: placing at the front/to the fore

Free verse: poetry which is unrhymed and without form

Hyperbole: (from the Greek for 'throwing too far') emphasis by exaggeration

Iambic pentameter: 10 syllable lines organised into five groups of two syllables – one unstressed, one stressed – diDUM diDUM diDUM diDUM diDUM.

Imagery: words used to create a picture or sensation, through **metaphor, simile** or other figurative language. Usually **visual** imagery - something seen in the mind's eye – but also
auditory imagery - represents a sound
olfactory imagery - a smell
gustatory imagery - a taste
tactile imagery - touch, for example hardness, softness, wetness, heat, cold

In media res: in the middle of things

Irony: (from the Greek for 'dissembling') irony consists of saying one thing when you mean another. Irony is achieved through understatement, concealment and allusion, rather than by direct statement.

Juxtaposition: two things placed close together with contrasting effect.

Lament: passionate expression of grief or sorrow

Lexical field: set of words

Narrator or **Speaker**: one telling the story, the **narrative.**

Metaphor: in metaphor, one thing is compared to another without using the linking words like or as, so it is more direct than a simile. One thing is actually said to be the other eg *My brother is a pig. The man is an ass.* Verbs can also be used metaphorically: *love blossoms.* Metaphors create new ways of looking at familiar objects and are often found in everyday speech eg *the root of the problem.*

Mimesis: imitation

Narrative: story

Narrative viewpoint: there are two main narrative viewpoints. In a **first person narrative**, the narrator is a character in the story who retells his or her first hand account of events. In a **third person narrative**, the narrative voice stands outside the story and is not a character. This type of narrative voice tends to be more objective and often is omniscient (that is, all seeing) and able to show the reader the thoughts of all the characters.

Onomatopoeia: where words sound like the things they describe eg *hiss, crash, murmur, creak.*

Oxymoron: a figure of speech that combines two contradictory terms eg *bitter sweet, living death, wise fool.*

Pathetic fallacy: the attribution of human feelings and responses to the natural world eg sullen clouds

Paradox: (from the Greek for 'beside-opinion') an apparently self contradictory statement, or a statement that seems in conflict with logic or opinion. Lying behind this superficial absurdity, however, is a meaning or a truth.

Perspective: point of view

Personification: a form of figurative language in which animals, inanimate objects and abstract ideas are addressed or described as if they were human eg *The breeze whispered gently. The trees waved their tops.*

Power words: words that have a powerful effect in a text.

Quatrain: group of four lines

Refrain: repeated line or lines – like a chorus in a song.

Reported speech: words reportedly spoken, not within speech marks eg He said that he had been crying.

Semantic field: group of words linked by meaning – see **Lexical set**.

Sestet: group of six lines

Sibilance: the recurrence of sounds known as sibilants which hiss - s, sh, zh, c, ch - eg *Ships that pass in the night, and speak each other in passing*

Simile: in a simile, one thing is compared to another using the linking words *like* or *as* eg *as big as a giant; he smoked like a chimney*

Sonnet: 14 lines of ten syllables with a defined rhyme scheme

Structural pivot: turning point

Symbol/symbolism: a symbol is a person, place, or thing that comes to represent an abstract idea or concept -- it is anything that stands for something beyond itself. Symbols are often universally understood eg green = jealousy; poppy = remembrance; cross = sacrifice. Linked to **metaphor** but not quite the same – a metaphor is more consciously creative and original.

Syndetic list: list with 'and' between the items.

Printed in Great Britain
by Amazon